AROUND the WORLD
Quilting Designs

Joyce Mori

American Quilter's Society
P. O. Box 3290 • Paducah, KY 42002-3290
www.AmericanQuilter.com

Located in Paducah, Kentucky, the American Quilter's Society (AQS) is dedicated to promoting the accomplishments of today's quilters. Through its publications and events, AQS strives to honor today's quiltmakers and their work and to inspire future creativity and innovation in quiltmaking.

EDITOR: SHELLEY HAWKINS
COPY EDITOR: CHRYSTAL ABHALTER
GRAPHIC DESIGN: ELAINE WILSON
COVER DESIGN: MICHAEL BUCKINGHAM
PHOTOGRAPHY: CHARLES R. LYNCH

Library of Congress Cataloging-in-Publication Data
Mori, Joyce.
    Around the world quilting designs / by Joyce Mori.
        p. cm.
    Summary: "Quilting designs inspired by sources from 20,000 BC to twentieth century such as an Egyptian mummy case, marble floors of Venetian churches, an Inuit wood mask, and Australian aboriginal art. Designs and patterns can be adapted to redwork embroidery and hand or machine appliqué"--Provided by publisher.
    ISBN 1-57432-893-X
    1. Quilting--Patterns. I. Title.

    TT835.M6815 2005
    746.46'041--dc22

                          2005012809

Referenced material includes the following sources:
New Encyclopedia Britannica. Chicago: Encyclopedia Britannica, Inc, 2002.
World Book Encyclopedia. Chicago: World Book Company, 2001.

Additional copies of this book may be ordered from the American Quilter's Society, P.O. Box 3290, Paducah, KY 42002-3290; 800-626-5420 (orders only please); or online at www.AmericanQuilter.com. For all other inquiries, call 270-898-7903.

Dedication

This book was written for all quilters who look at the world around them as a source of inspiration and beauty. Objects from the world around me have served as a basis for the designs in this book, and I hope quilters will use both these designs and the designs they create to make joyful quilts.

Acknowledgments

I sincerely thank the American Quilter's Society for publishing six of my books. All of my editors have been pleasant and helpful to work with, and the graphic artists do a masterful job making my designs come to life.

I love my husband for supporting my quilting endeavors, and my daughter, Susan, for offering advice and ideas.

Contents

Introduction

Two of my previous books feature Native American quilting designs and this book is an expansion of the concept, featuring quilting designs from cultures all over the world. It has been enjoyable and challenging to collect the designs, adapt them, and offer them to quilters.

The motifs not only span the globe, they also cross the centuries. When the information was available, I provided the approximate age of the designs, which are organized by continent and cultural group.

Because many quilters trace their heritage and make family quilts to recognize ancestors, I hope these quilting motifs will be helpful in your family memory quilts. No matter how many different cultural groups, countries, or geographical regions are represented in your background, I believe you can find some designs in this book that relate to your heritage.

The designs can also be used in a quilt that reflects a wonderful trip you took out of the country. Motifs from exotic locales have been included for those of you that are intrepid world-wide travelers. Of course, the designs are wonderful on their own without any link to a geographic region or ancestral heritage.

Longarm quilting is one of the fastest growing areas in our hobby, so I included a few continuous-line designs. Theresa Fleming, a longarm quilter from Colorado, has taken some of my motifs and converted them into designs for both shortarm and longarm quilters. In several instances, there is more than one variation shown for a motif. A single motif is also provided for quilters who do not wish to use the continuous-line designs as such.

Upon completing your next quilt top, consider using some of these quilting designs to enhance and add special meaning to your project. Use a copy machine to reduce or enlarge designs as needed. If you reduce a design significantly, you may need to omit some lines to make quilting easier. Likewise, enlarging a design may create blank spaces in a motif in which you may add lines to fill the area.

Some of the designs can be adapted to redwork-type embroidery and hand or machine appliqué. They can also be scanned into your computer and converted to machine embroidery motifs, and a few of them can be used as quilt labels. I hope you will take advantage of the many possibilities these designs offer.

Design Inspiration

All of my designs are inspired by the objects and patterns found in craft pieces of the past. I work in the long tradition of artists who draw inspiration from the world around them. Since my college days, I have visited museums and museum collections in storage around the country, photographing and sketching objects that appeal to me.

I like to observe objects of all sorts, including pottery textiles, leather, wood, stone, etc., and see how they can be a source of inspiration for my work. While looking at an object, I study its shape and individual motifs, not the entire design. I might find a leaf, flower, or general set of lines that will work into a great quilting design. I isolate the unit that appeals to me and redraw it for my use. It is probably true that if five quilters looked at the same object, they would each isolate a different part of the design.

After isolating a unit, I place it in a suitable format, such as multiples of four, six, or eight. It might be turned as much as 180 degrees. Then the design is likely to be modified further. Perhaps some lines are added or subtracted. A designer must think about how a design looks as well as whether it is too difficult to quilt. Connecting lines may be drawn between the units.

Quilters can study a teapot, furniture, sled, jewelry, or most anything they like and reproduce or manipulate a simplified version of the piece to create a quilting design. The shape of a piece can also be used as a design. Additional sources for designs include books, especially older ones. Books or magazines with antique collections, books of old Victorian wrought-iron decorations, publications of folk-art pieces, and collections of ancient artifacts are useful design sources.

Artisans have used similar methods through the ages. Folk artists study old toys, lithographs, textile arts, and Pennsylvania frakturs to reproduce similar motifs in their folk-art patterns. Native American women took Jacobean crewel designs that were shown to them by nuns and used the motifs in their quill and beadwork. Native American tribes borrowed motifs from each other and used them as is or combined them in new ways.

If you have an antique piece that has been handed down in your family, it can be a rewarding process to take a part of that design to create your own quilting design. It is another way to maintain a connection with your ancestors.

Designs from Africa

Africa is the second most populous continent, with 825 million people and a population growth rate of three percent per year. It encompasses one-fifth of the world's land area. Africa is divided in half by the equator, so a tropical or desert climate is prevalent. The Sahara, Namib, and Kalahari are the major desert areas. The East African Rift System is the continent's most extensive mountain system. Africa contains 53 independent countries and over 800 ethnic groups. Black Africans, Arabs, and Berbers are the major groups of people.

Copper, diamonds, gold, and petroleum make up the mineral wealth of this continent. However, agriculture is the major economic activity, even though only six percent of the continent is arable. Two-thirds of all Africans live in rural areas.

Over 5,000 years ago, the Egyptian civilization could be found along the Nile River. There were several empires based on trade that developed throughout Africa from the fifth century to colonial times. In the late 1400s and early 1500s, Europeans began to establish themselves in Africa, and by the early 1900s, the continent had been divided into colonial empires by various European countries. Beginning in 1950 and continuing in the 1980s, many of these colonies gained independence.

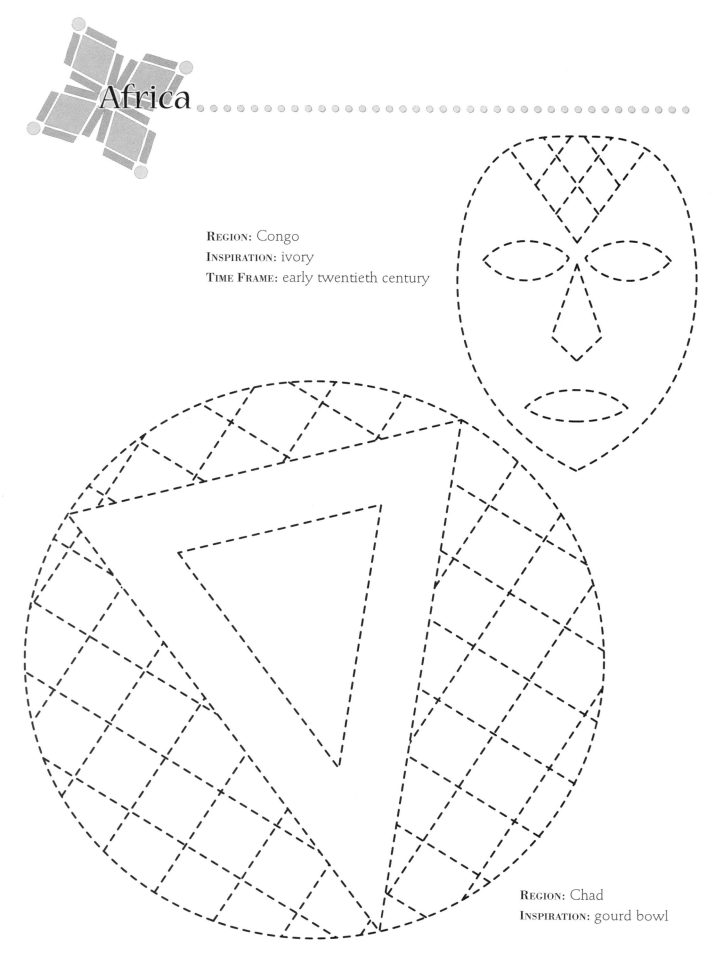

Africa

REGION: Congo
INSPIRATION: ivory
TIME FRAME: early twentieth century

REGION: Chad
INSPIRATION: gourd bowl

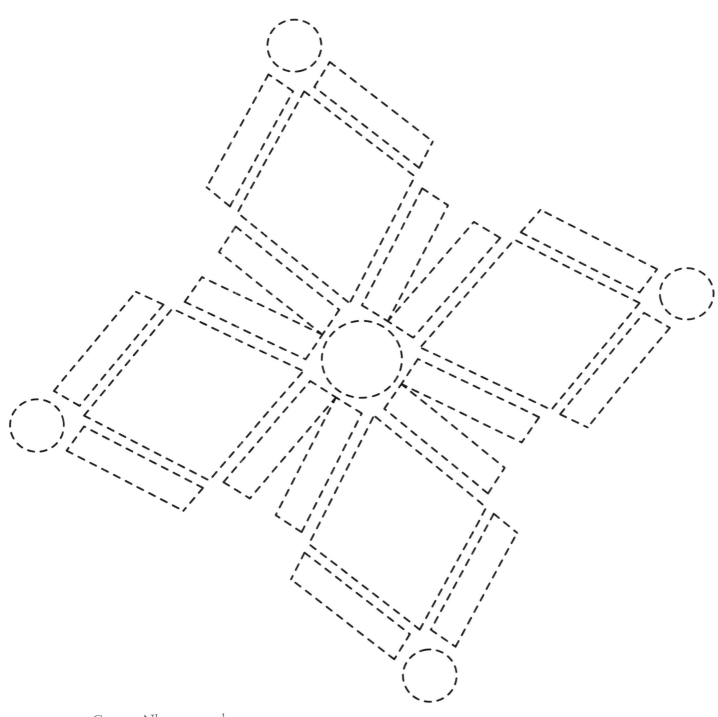

REGION: Congo, Nkanu people
INSPIRATION: wood panel

Africa

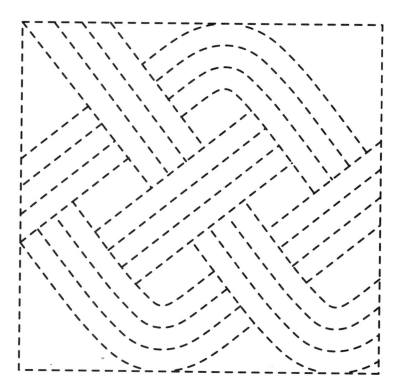

REGION: Bakuba, Congo
INSPIRATION: wooden cup

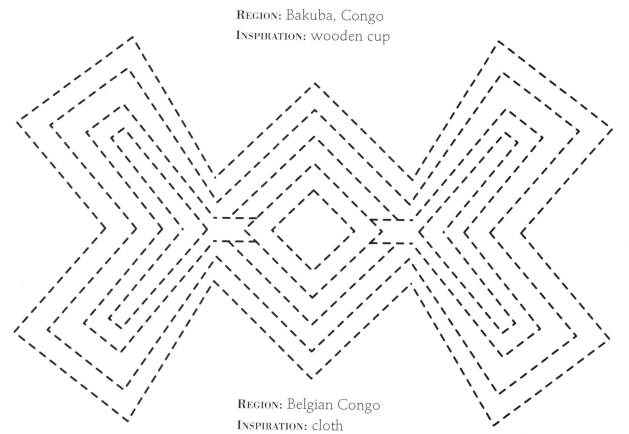

REGION: Belgian Congo
INSPIRATION: cloth

REGION: Egypt

INSPIRATION: tomb mural at Thebes

TIME FRAME: 1570–1320 BC

Africa

REGION: Egypt

INSPIRATION: painted design from a mummy case

TIME FRAME: 1085–332 BC

REGION: Egypt
INSPIRATION: gilded mummy case
TIME FRAME: 300 BC

REGION: Egypt
INSPIRATION: gilded mummy case
TIME FRAME: 300 BC

Africa

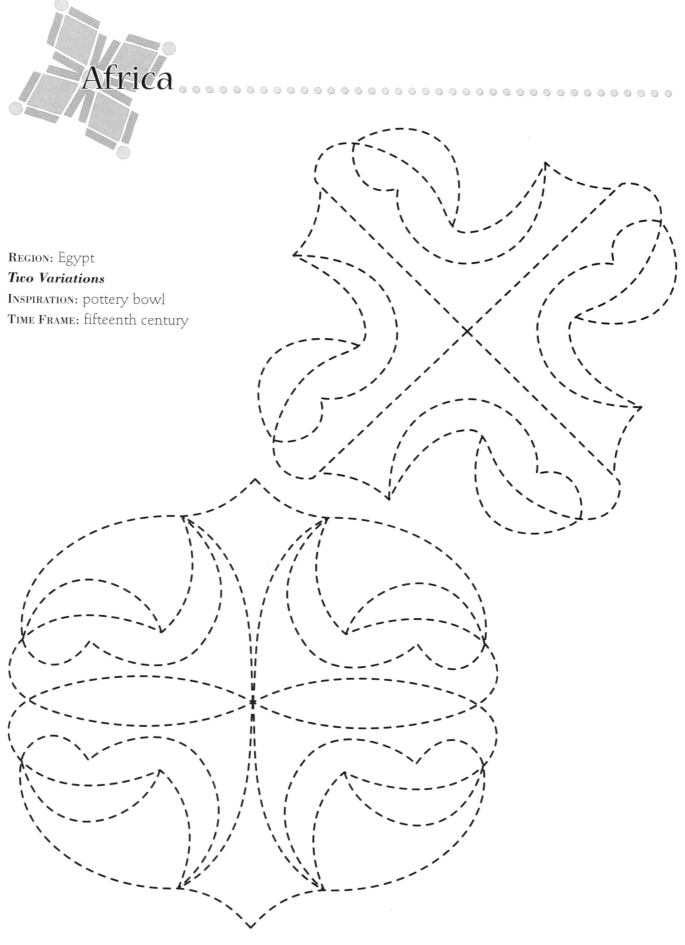

REGION: Egypt

Two Variations

INSPIRATION: pottery bowl

TIME FRAME: fifteenth century

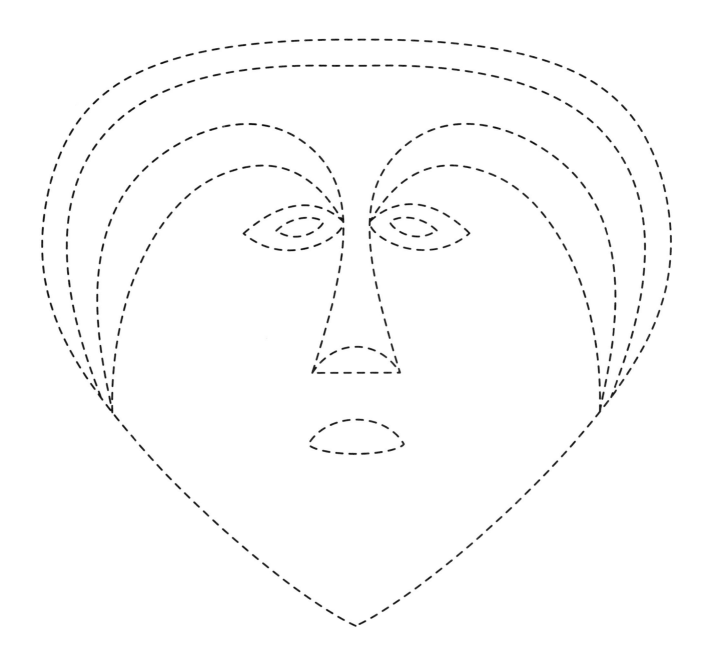

REGION: Gabon, Fang Tribe

INSPIRATION: heart-shaped wooden dance mask

Africa

REGION: Gabon, Kota people
INSPIRATION: brass and copper guardian figure

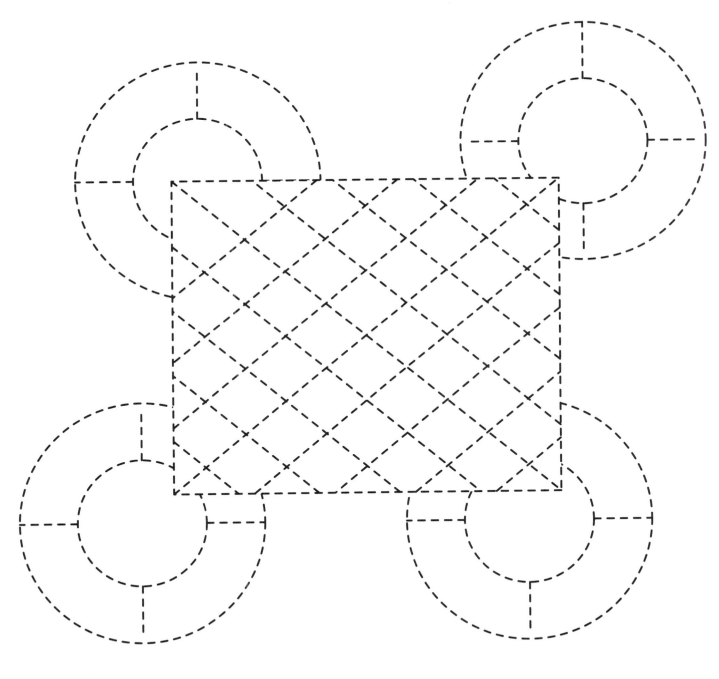

REGION: Ghana

INSPIRATION: cloth

Africa

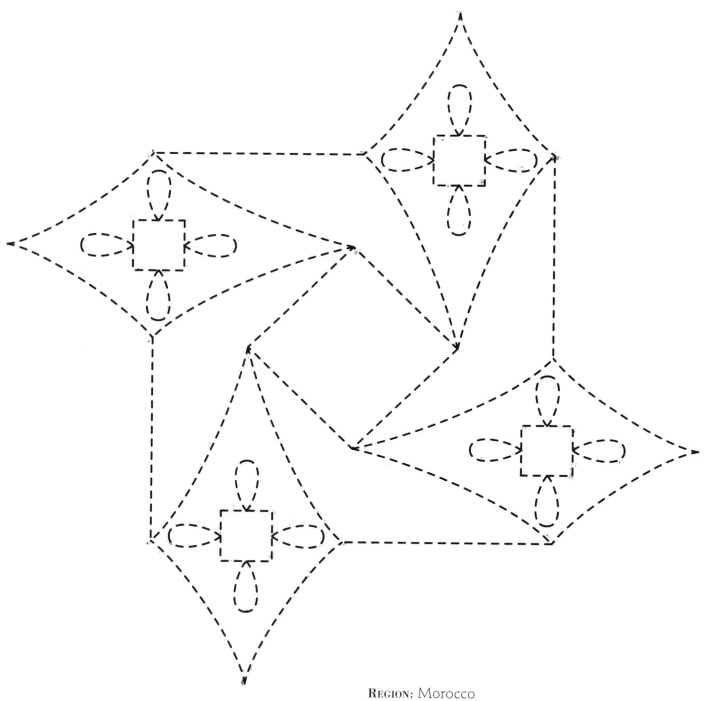

REGION: Morocco
INSPIRATION: ceramic piece

REGION: Tangier, Morocco
INSPIRATION: lute

Africa

REGION: Northern Congo
INSPIRATION: wall painting

REGION: Zanzibar

INSPIRATION: carved door

Designs from Asia

Asia is the largest continent in landmass and population, with one-third of the world's land surface and three-fifths of the world's population. The population growth rate is two percent per year. Over 3½ billion people live in Asia. Siberia, Central Asia, and parts of Southwestern Asia are sparsely populated, but India and East Asia have two-thirds of the total Asian population. Asia contains 49 countries, including China, Asian Russia, Saudi Arabia, Thailand, Japan, the Philippines, Taiwan, and Indonesia.

The continent has the highest point in the world of 29,035 feet at Mount Everest, and the lowest at 1,310 feet below sea level in the Dead Sea. The Caspian Sea, which is the world's largest body of inland water, is located in Asia. Fifteen percent of the land is arable and more than 50 percent of the population is involved in agriculture. Fish is a major source of protein for the people.

The climate ranges include polar cold, dry deserts, and hot-and-humid tropical areas. In the area known as the Fertile Crescent (the valley of Tigris and Euphrates), archaeologists have found evidence of the world's first civilization. This civilization had one of the earliest uses of writing. Other civilizations occurred in the Indus, Huang He, and Yangtze valleys.

Around 1750, European countries began conquering large parts of Asia, but by the 1900s, most of the regions had gained their independence. The people practice a variety of religions, including Buddhism, Christianity, Confucianism, Hinduism, Islam, and Shinto.

REGION: Borneo
INSPIRATION: Dyak wooden shield

REGION: Asia Minor
INSPIRATION: plate
TIME FRAME: 1500–1600

Continuous-line Pattern

Asia

REGION: China

INSPIRATION: bronze ritual wine container

TIME FRAME: 1200–1100 BC

REGION: China
INSPIRATION: calligraphy motif

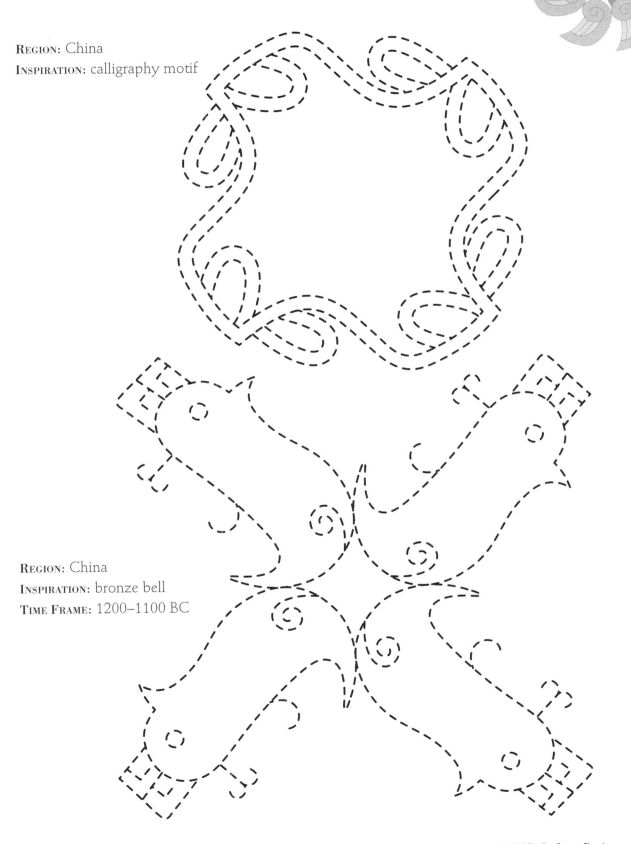

REGION: China
INSPIRATION: bronze bell
TIME FRAME: 1200–1100 BC

Asia

REGION: China

INSPIRATION: bronze canteen with silver inlay

TIME FRAME: 300–250 BC

REGION: China

INSPIRATION: bronze and gold mirror

TIME FRAME: 600–800 AD

Continuous-line Pattern

REGION: India

INSPIRATION: silk embroidery on cotton sash

TIME FRAME: late seventeenth century

Designed by Theresa Fleming

Asia

REGION: Bali, Indonesia
INSPIRATION: painted wooden piece

REGION: Bali, Indonesia
INSPIRATION: painted wooden animal

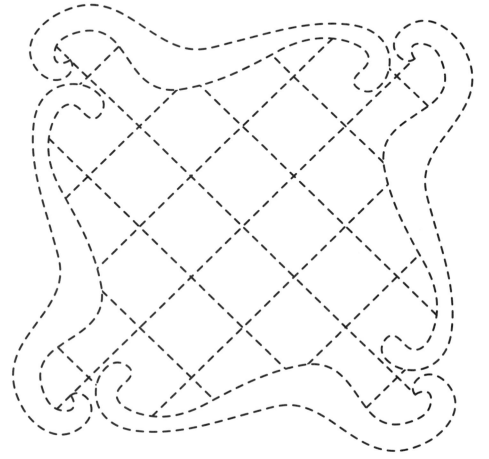

REGION: Sulawesi, Indonesia
INSPIRATION: cards

Asia

REGION: Iran or Afghanistan
INSPIRATION: earthenware plate
TIME FRAME: tenth century

REGION: Iraq

INSPIRATION: glazed bowl

TIME FRAME: ninth century

Asia

REGION: Japan

INSPIRATION: incense container

TIME FRAME: eighteenth century

REGION: Iraq

INSPIRATION: jar

TIME FRAME: tenth century

REGION: Korea

INSPIRATION: porcelain jar

TIME FRAME: nineteenth century

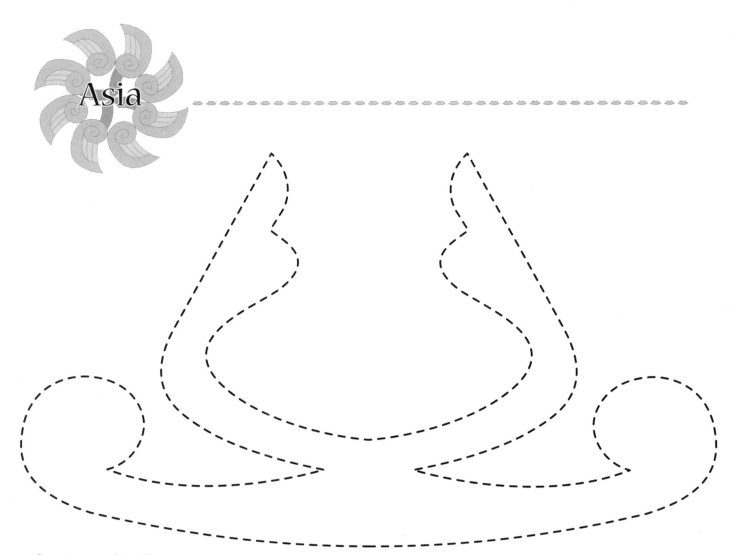

Continuous-line Pattern

REGION: Mesopotamia

INSPIRATION: pottery bowl

TIME FRAME: eleventh to twelfth century

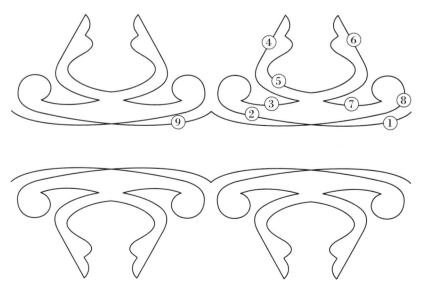

Designed by Theresa Fleming

REGION: Persia

INSPIRATION: wall tile

TIME FRAME: fourteenth century

REGION: Samarra, a city on the Tigris River

INSPIRATION: panel

TIME FRAME: ninth century

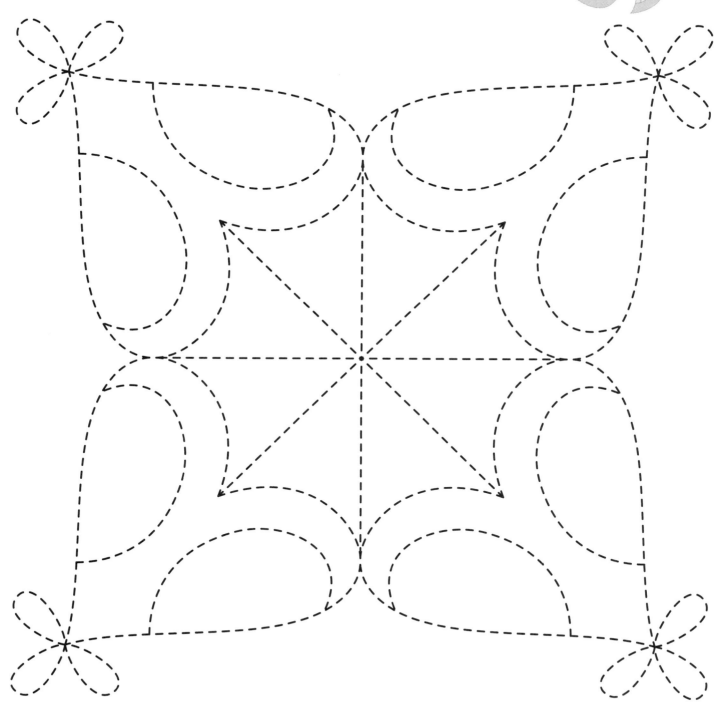

REGION: Syria

INSPIRATION: brass object with silver inlay

TIME FRAME: late fifteenth or sixteenth century

REGION: Turkey

INSPIRATION: carafe

TIME FRAME: 1545–1550

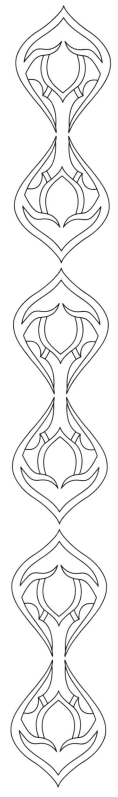

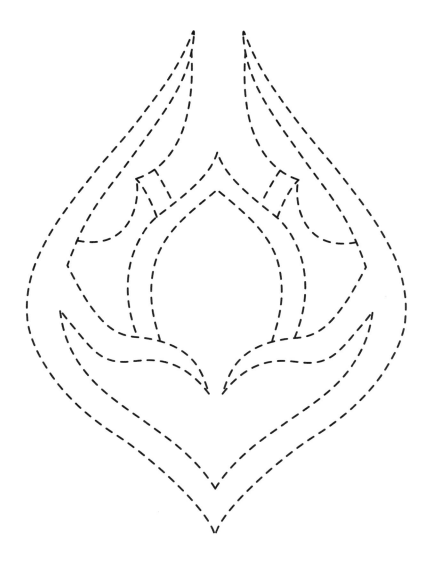

REGION: Anatolia, Turkey
INSPIRATION: Iznik pot lid
TIME FRAME: ca. 1560

Border Design

Asia

Design Variation

REGION: Vietnam
INSPIRATION: stoneware jar
TIME FRAME: fifteenth century

Designs from Australia

The Australian continent is an island that includes the island of Tasmania. It is the smallest continent. The phrase "down under" is often used in reference to Australia, because it is entirely in the Southwestern Hemisphere. The country's interior is very dry and unable to support a large population.

The Aborigines have lived in Australia for about 65,000 years, originally migrating from Southeastern Asia. They were the native population, but now are the largest non-white minority, making up only about one percent of the population.

The Dutch came to Australia in 1616 and the British arrived in 1688. In 1770, James Cook claimed Australia for Britain. Beginning in 1788, Australia was a British prison colony. Today, most of the people are of British or Irish ancestry. From the 1960s, immigration rules relaxed and many Asians have arrived in the country.

Christianity is the major religion and English is the official language. The mineral wealth of Australia includes bauxite, iron ore, coal, petroleum, natural gas, uranium, and diamonds.

Australia

REGION: Australia

INSPIRATION: Aboriginal shield

TIME FRAME: nineteenth century

REGION: Australia

INSPIRATION: Aboriginal art from a tjuringa

Border Design

Australia

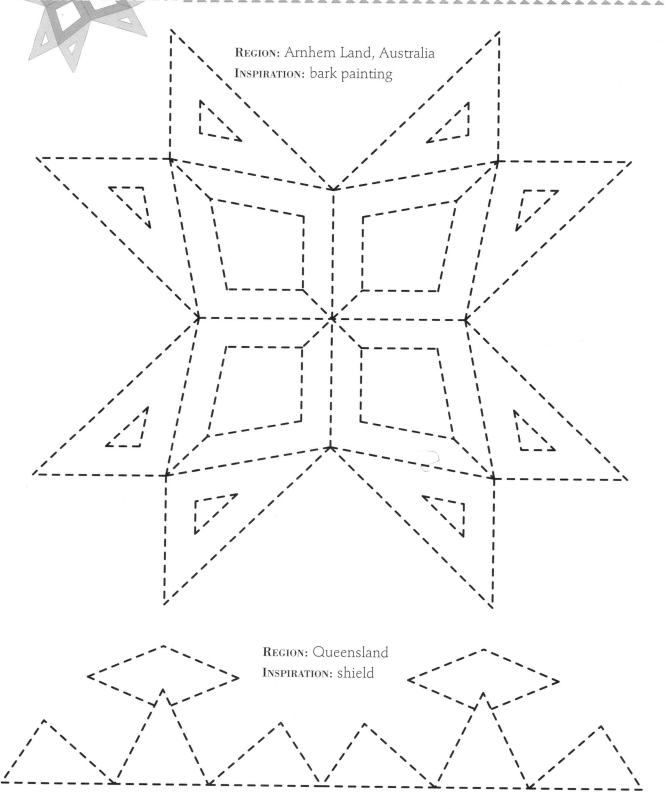

REGION: Arnhem Land, Australia
INSPIRATION: bark painting

REGION: Queensland
INSPIRATION: shield

REGION: Sydney, Australia
INSPIRATION: cast ironwork
TIME FRAME: late 1800s

Australia

REGION: Sydney, Australia
INSPIRATION: cast ironwork
TIME FRAME: late 1800s

REGION: Sydney, Australia
INSPIRATION: cast ironwork
TIME FRAME: late 1800s

Designs from Europe

Europe has one-eighth of the world's population, but it is the second smallest continent in landmass. One-third of Europe is arable. The continent is composed of 47 countries, including European Russia. Just a few of the many other countries include Bulgaria, England, Finland, France, Germany, Ireland, Italy, Norway, Portugal, Spain, Sweden, and Ukraine. A variety of climates can be found, from tundra to subtropical and semiarid. The Alpine Mountain system extends from Spain to the Caspian Sea.

The second most densely populated continent, Europe has the lowest rate of population increase. The tiny country of the Netherlands is one of the world's most densely populated countries with 1,000 people per square mile. Over 60 separate languages are spoken. The Protestant Reformation of the 1500s broke the dominance of the Roman Catholic Church, but Christianity is the major religion of the people.

Two early civilizations in the region were the Greeks and Romans, dating from 3000 BC. The Renaissance of the fifteenth and early sixteenth centuries was a revival of Greek and Roman classical learning that started Europe on a path of modern development in science and worldwide exploration. The development of ruling monarchies began in the sixteenth century and lasted until the early 1800s when democratic movements became widespread. Since the 1800s, 60 million Europeans have emigrated from the continent. Europe is a major industrial region, with a high standard of living in Western Europe.

Europe

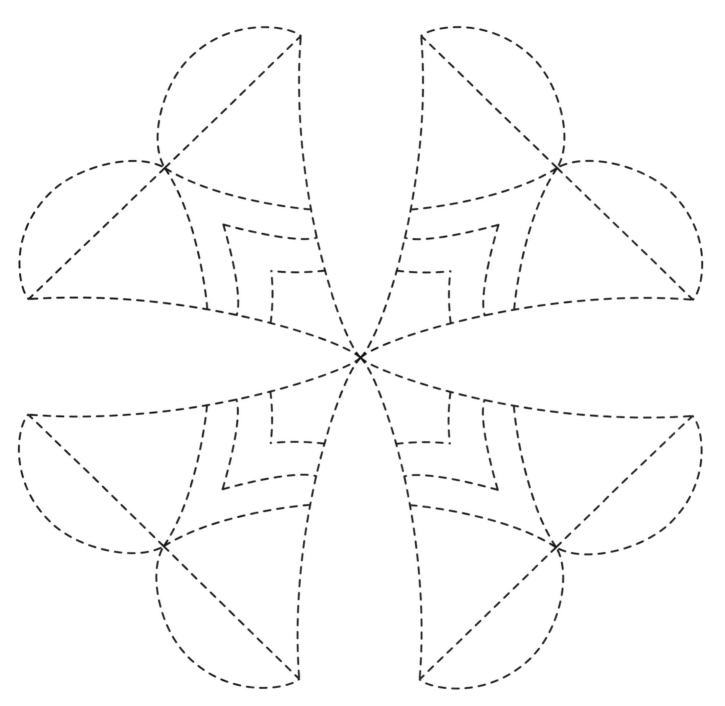

REGION: Crete

INSPIRATION: Minoan terracotta chest

TIME FRAME: mid-thirteenth century BC

REGION: England

INSPIRATION: needlework carpet

TIME FRAME: mid-nineteenth century

REGION: England

INSPIRATION: bronze Celtic horse head mount

TIME FRAME: mid-to-late first century

Europe

REGION: France

INSPIRATION: Celtic gold-plated bronze disc

REGION: France
INSPIRATION: wall panel
TIME FRAME: late 1600s

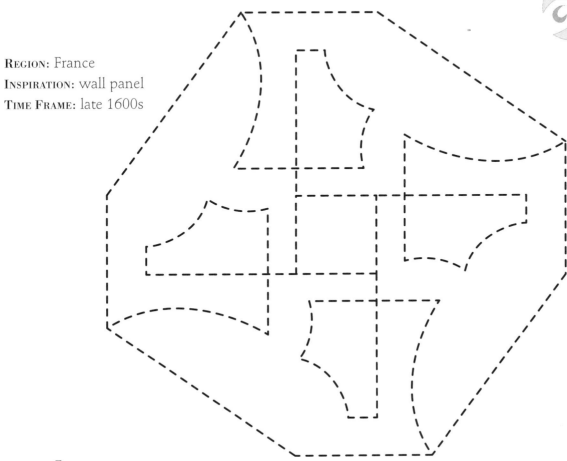

REGION: France
INSPIRATION: limestone architectural frieze
TIME FRAME: mid-twelfth century

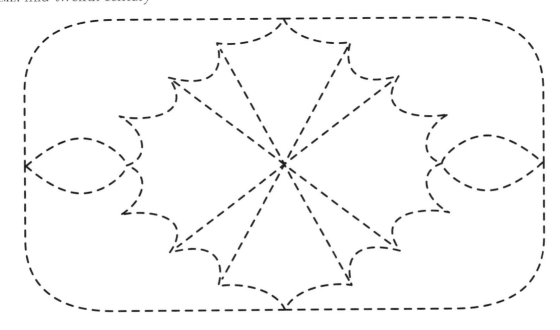

Europe

REGION: Great Britain

INSPIRATION: bronze mirror

TIME FRAME: beginning of the Christian era

REGION: Venice, Italy

INSPIRATION: marble floor, Church of Santilario

TIME FRAME: ninth century

REGION: Italy
INSPIRATION: majolica pottery
TIME FRAME: 1500

Europe

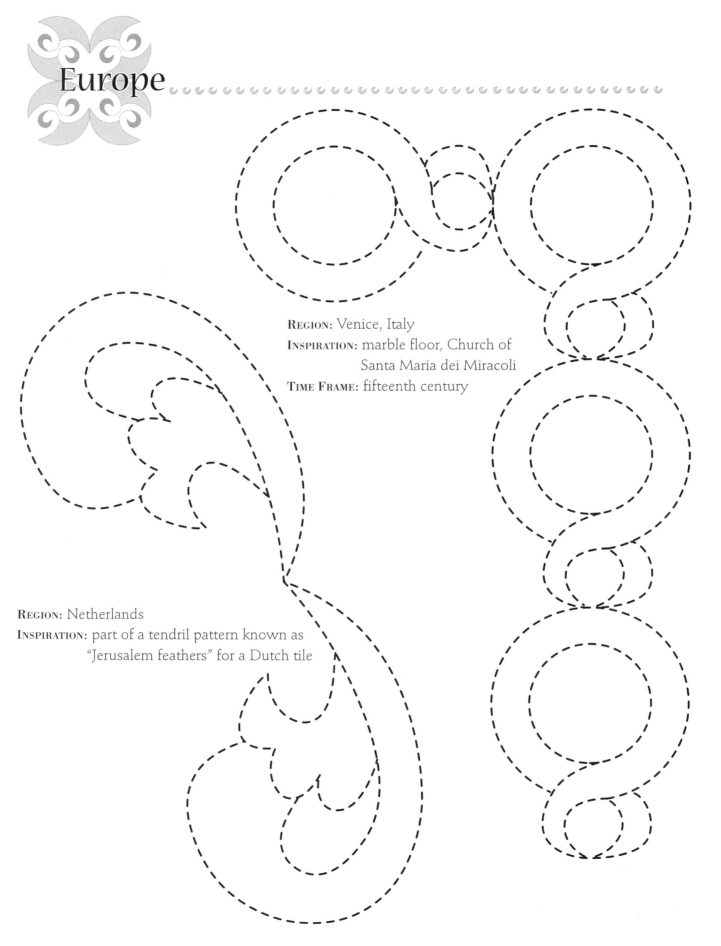

REGION: Venice, Italy
INSPIRATION: marble floor, Church of
Santa Maria dei Miracoli
TIME FRAME: fifteenth century

REGION: Netherlands
INSPIRATION: part of a tendril pattern known as
"Jerusalem feathers" for a Dutch tile

REGION: Netherlands
INSPIRATION: Dutch tile

Europe

Continuous-line Pattern

REGION: Norway

INSPIRATION: painted chest

Designed by Theresa Fleming

REGION: Russia

INSPIRATION: wooden door

TIME FRAME: 1890s

Europe

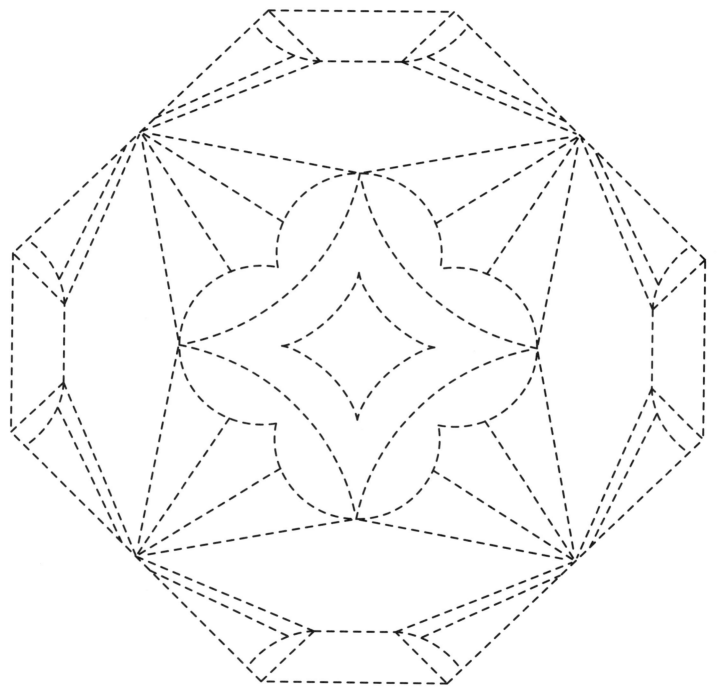

REGION: Russia

INSPIRATION: cupboard

TIME FRAME: early 1900s

REGION: Scandinavia
INSPIRATION: mirror
TIME FRAME: Bronze Age

REGION: Scandinavia
INSPIRATION: bronze razor
TIME FRAME: Bronze Age

Europe

REGION: Spain

INSPIRATION: bowl

TIME FRAME: late fifteenth century

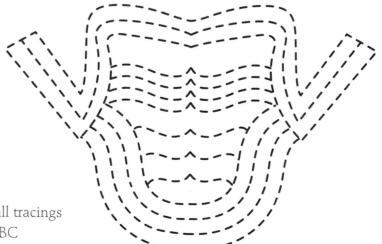

REGION: Spain

INSPIRATION: cave wall tracings

TIME FRAME: 20,000 BC

Designs from
North America

The North American continent has a population of 480 million. It ranks fourth in population and third in landmass when compared to the other continents. Mexico, the Caribbean, and Central America have one-third of the continent's population and high birth rates. Their population growth is two or three times that of the United States of America. North America includes Greenland, Canada, the United States, Mexico, Central America, and the Caribbean Islands. There are 23 countries in all.

The continent has the most varied climate of any continent, from Arctic cold to deserts and tropical rain forests. However, the major climate type is temperate. The Mississippi River basin and its tributaries, such as the Missouri and Ohio rivers, cover more than one-eighth of the total continent area.

This region exports more food than any other continent. One-eighth of the land is arable making the continent among the world's most productive. Great wealth can be found in the United States, and unfortunately much poverty in Central America.

The earliest North American inhabitants arrived from Asia 15,000 to 35,000 years ago. The great civilizations of the continent were the Aztec, Maya, Olmec, and Toltec. These civilizations were in Central America and Mexico in the 1400s and early 1500s. Europeans arrived around this time. In the United States, settlers and colonizers gradually took over, removing Native Americans and placing them on isolated reservations, mostly west of the Mississippi.

More than one-third of people in the United States and one-half of the people in Canada have ancestors from England, Ireland, Scotland, or Wales. One-quarter of all Canadians have French ancestors. In Central America and Mexico, most European ancestry is Spanish.

REGION: British Columbia, Canada

INSPIRATION: Native American, Kwakiutl tribe, wooden mask

TIME FRAME: 1880

Border Design

Design Variation

REGION: Canada

INSPIRATION: armoire

TIME FRAME: eighteenth century

North America

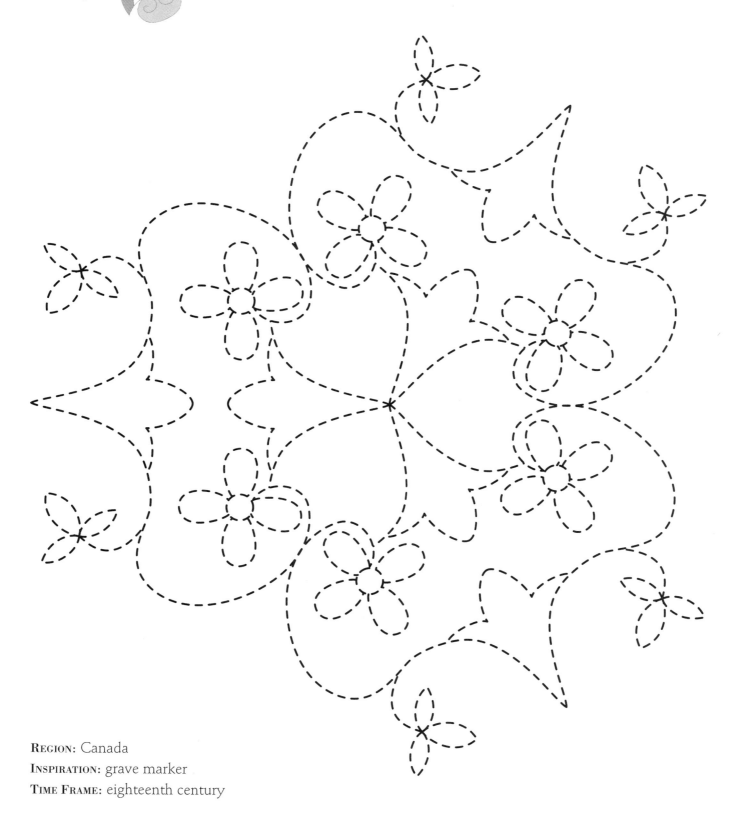

REGION: Canada

INSPIRATION: grave marker

TIME FRAME: eighteenth century

REGION: Canada

INSPIRATION: painted motif on a buffet

TIME FRAME: early twentieth century

REGION: Quebec, Canada

INSPIRATION: Native American, Huron, dyed
moose-hair embroidery design
on moccasins

TIME FRAME: 1825

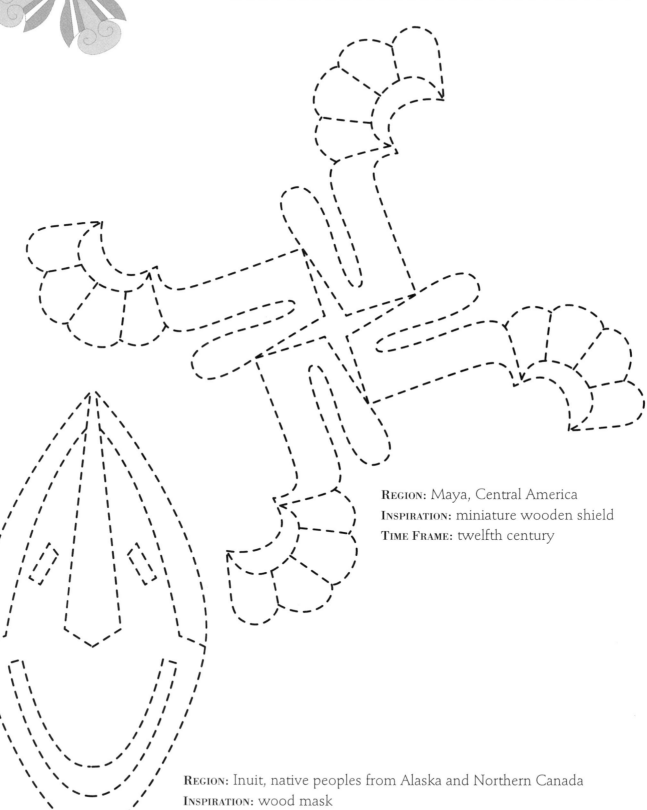

REGION: Maya, Central America
INSPIRATION: miniature wooden shield
TIME FRAME: twelfth century

REGION: Inuit, native peoples from Alaska and Northern Canada
INSPIRATION: wood mask

REGION: Mexico

INSPIRATION: Mixtec pottery

TIME FRAME: 900–1494

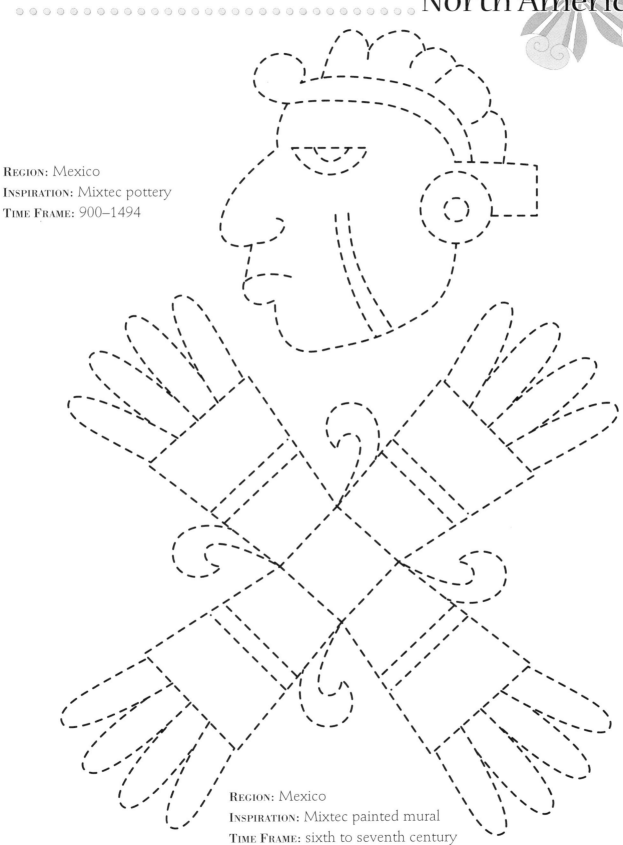

REGION: Mexico

INSPIRATION: Mixtec painted mural

TIME FRAME: sixth to seventh century

REGION: Mexico
INSPIRATION: Olmec axe

Design Variation

REGION: Yucatán, Mexico
INSPIRATION: Chichén Itzá mural
TIME FRAME: twelfth century

REGION: Zapotec, Mexico
INSPIRATION: palace wall decoration at Mitla

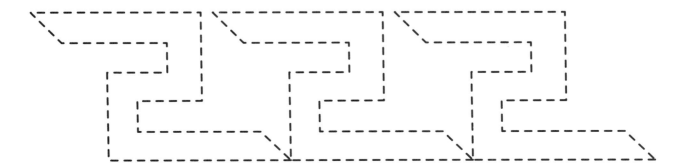

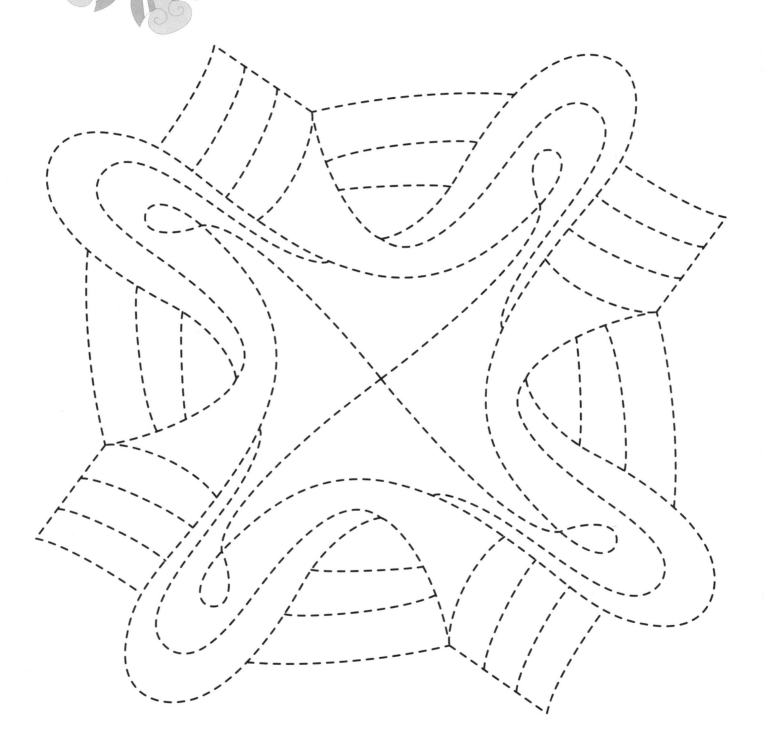

REGION: Tennessee, United States

INSPIRATION: Native American stamped pottery

TIME FRAME: 1500–2000 years ago, middle to late Woodland period

REGION: United States

INSPIRATION: combination of flowers from a Pennsylvania Dutch fractur (paper document) and architectural detail on a Victorian-style house window

TIME FRAME: fractur – 1810

North America

REGION: United States

INSPIRATION: Pennsylvania German plate

TIME FRAME: 1825–1835

REGION: United States

INSPIRATION: Pennsylvania German wooden chest design

North America

REGION: United States
INSPIRATION: home architectural detail
TIME FRAME: 1864

REGION: New Orleans, Louisiana, United States
INSPIRATION: wrought-iron gate

REGION: Charleston, South Carolina, United States
INSPIRATION: wrought-iron railing

REGION: United States

INSPIRATION: stamped embroidery design

TIME FRAME: 1917

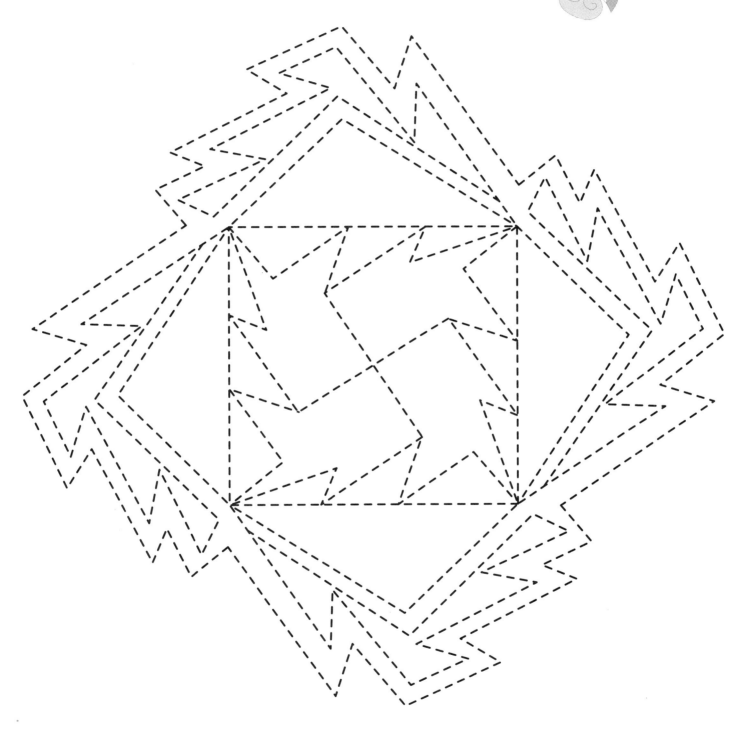

REGION: Southwestern United States
INSPIRATION: Mimbres bowl
TIME FRAME: prehistoric

North America

Region: United States
Inspiration: stamped embroidery design
Time frame: 1917

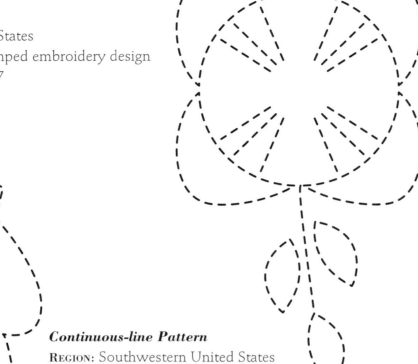

Continuous-line Pattern
Region: Southwestern United States
Inspiration: pottery vase

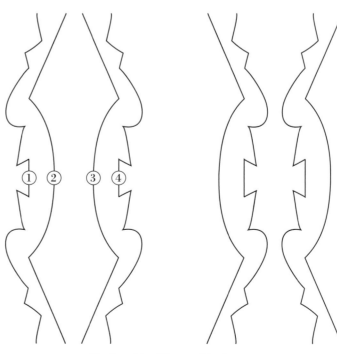

Designed by Theresa Fleming

Designs from the
Pacific Islands

Antarctica is one of the seven continents and it is buried in ice over 7,100 feet thick at the South Pole. Because the design possibilities from this area are limited, it was substituted with the Pacific Islands, also called Oceania. The cultural richness of the Pacific Islands is great, yielding many design inspirations for quilting motifs.

The Pacific Islands comprise the following three regions as denoted by anthropologists and geographers: Melanesia, Micronesia, and Polynesia. They cover about 500,000 square miles. New Guinea and New Zealand are the largest islands. Other well-known islands are Easter Island, Fiji, Guam, Hawaii, Marshall Islands, and Samoa. There are 14 million people living in the Pacific Islands, and most of the islands are densely populated, especially along the coasts. The climate is tropical except for New Zealand. Tourism is important to the economy of the region.

The first European explorer, Ferdinand Magellan, arrived in 1520. Other explorers and missionaries followed, and by the late 1800s, Europeans had established colonial influence and trade relations throughout the region.

REGION: Asmat, Dutch New Guinea
INSPIRATION: paddle blade

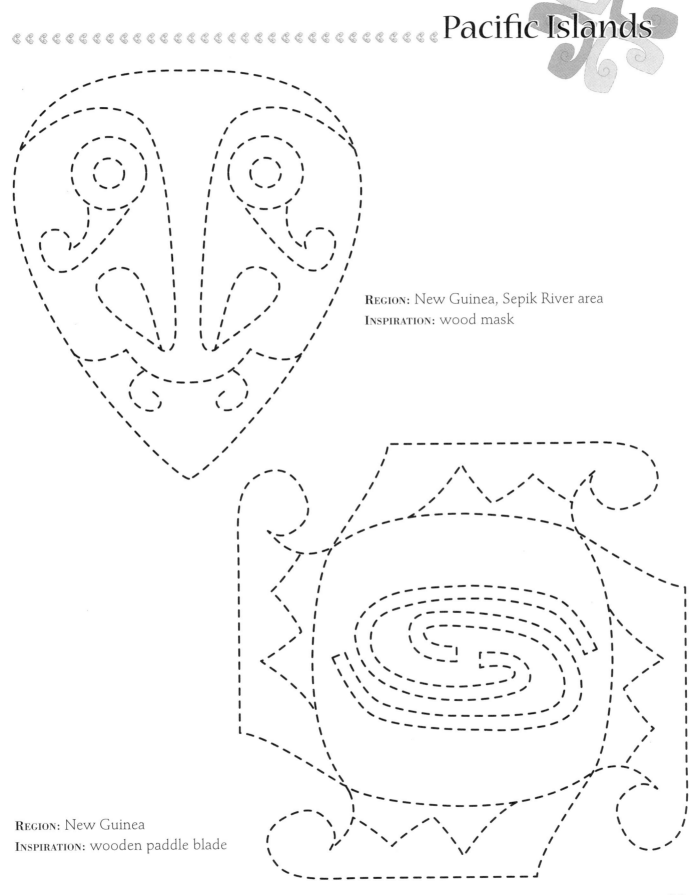

REGION: New Guinea, Sepik River area
INSPIRATION: wood mask

REGION: New Guinea
INSPIRATION: wooden paddle blade

Pacific Islands

Continuous-line Pattern

REGION: New Guinea, Sepik River area
INSPIRATION: wooden drum

REGION: New Zealand
INSPIRATION: Maori wood carvings

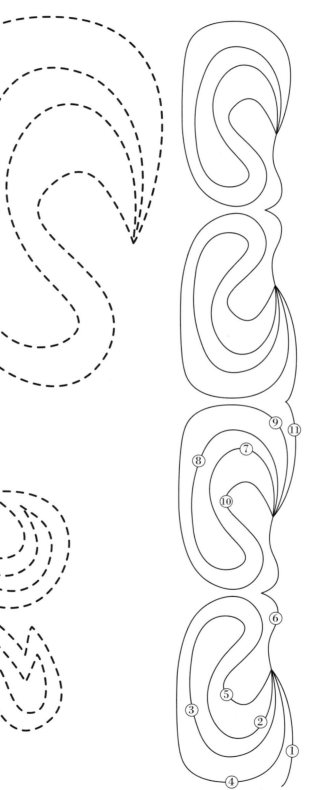

Designed by Theresa Fleming

REGION: New Guinea
INSPIRATION: wooden shield
TIME FRAME: late twentieth century

REGION: New Guinea
INSPIRATION: modern wooden shield

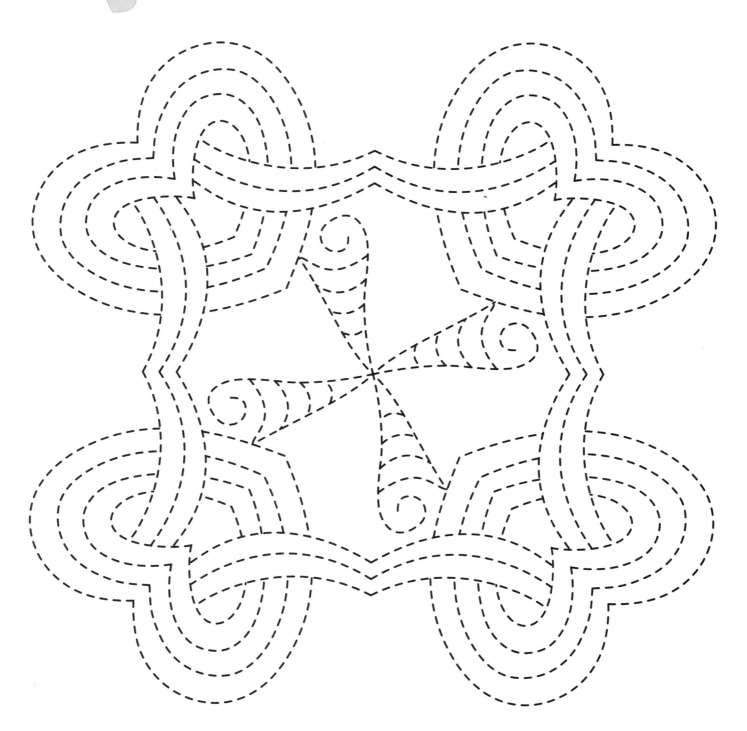

REGION: New Zealand

INSPIRATION: Maori wood carvings

Designed by Theresa Fleming

Continuous-line Pattern

REGION: New Zealand

INSPIRATION: Maori design

Design Variation

REGION: Oceania
INSPIRATION: war canoe

REGION: Melanesia
INSPIRATION: carved coconut shell

Designs from
South America

South America occupies 12 percent of the world's landmass and is the fourth largest continent. Seven percent of the land is arable, but agricultural productivity is low. One-fourth of the land is pasture and one-half is covered by forest, mainly the Amazon River forest. The Amazon River basin drains one-third of South America's land into the Atlantic. Lake Titicaca is on the border of Peru and Bolivia, and is the highest freshwater lake in the world, at 12,500 feet above sea level.

The climate includes the tropical rain forest in the Amazon River basin, the desert in Chile, and the Andes Mountains on the western side of the continent. However, most of the climate is tropical. A total of 12 countries make up South America. Most of these countries have a small class of landowners, factory owners, and military leaders that control the country and money. The majority of people are poor.

Six percent of the world's population is in South America. The original people were of Asiatic origin and arrived over 20,000 years ago. Columbus landed in South America in 1498. The Inca civilization was decimated when the region came under European control in 1535.

Spanish is the main language, but Portuguese is spoken in Brazil. Three other European languages are found in small pockets. Indian language speakers are mostly located in the Andes. Eighty-five percent of the people are Roman Catholic.

South America has a high population growth rate and one-half of the population resides in Brazil. The greatest density of population is along the coasts. Brazil is the economic power of the continent, but Argentina, Venezuela, Columbia, and Chile are trying to develop their economies.

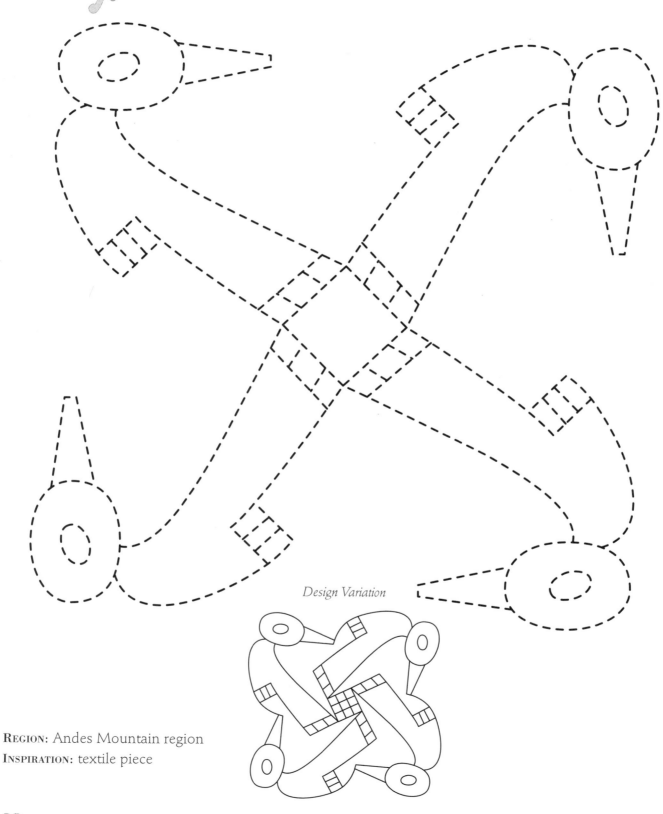

Design Variation

REGION: Andes Mountain region
INSPIRATION: textile piece

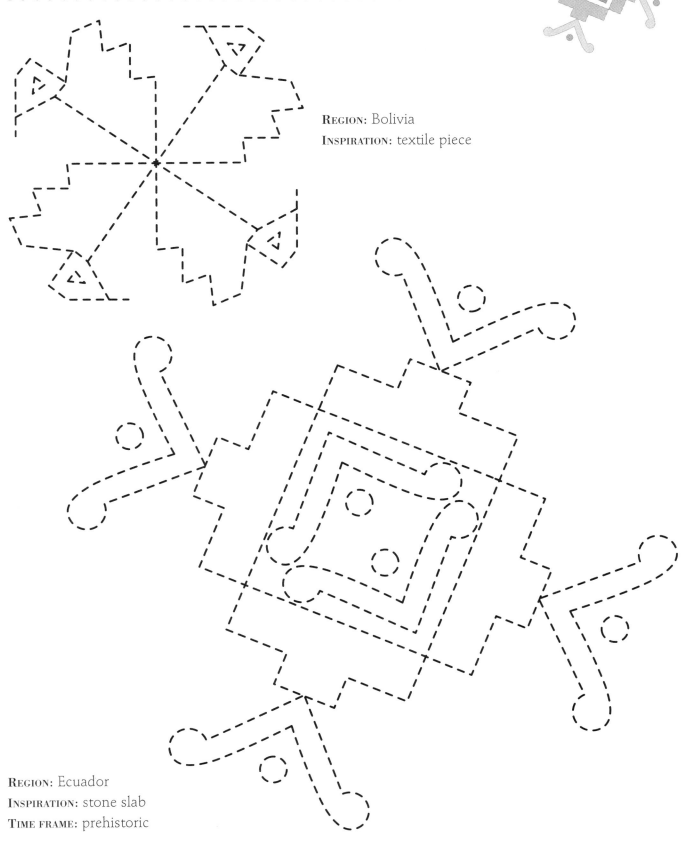

REGION: Bolivia
INSPIRATION: textile piece

REGION: Ecuador
INSPIRATION: stone slab
TIME FRAME: prehistoric

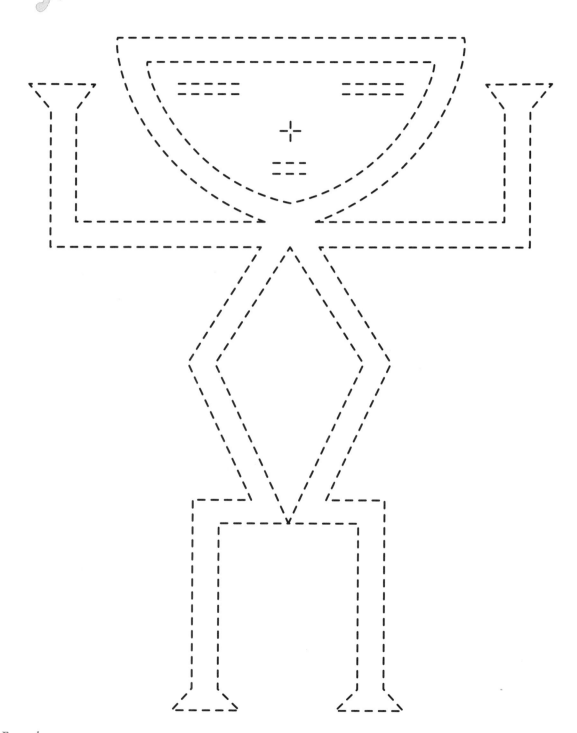

REGION: Ecuador

INSPIRATION: Milagro culture, gold ornament

REGION: Peru

INSPIRATION: Nazca pottery

Design Variation

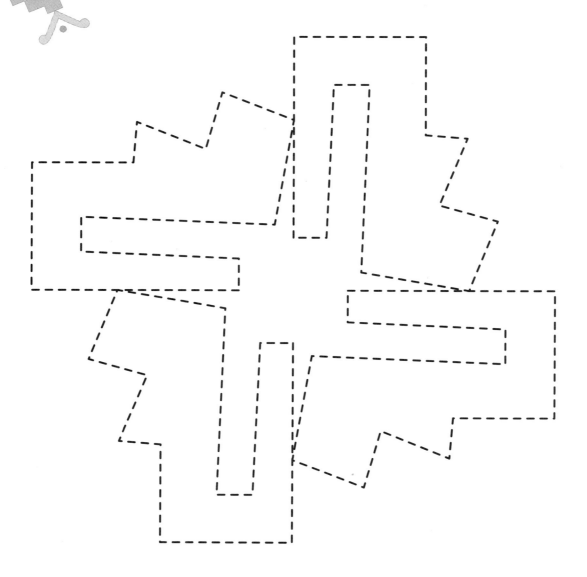

South America

Border Design

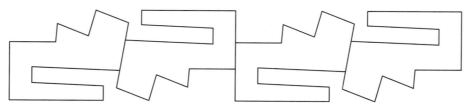

REGION: Peru
INSPIRATION: Nazca pitcher
TIME FRAME: AD 1–700

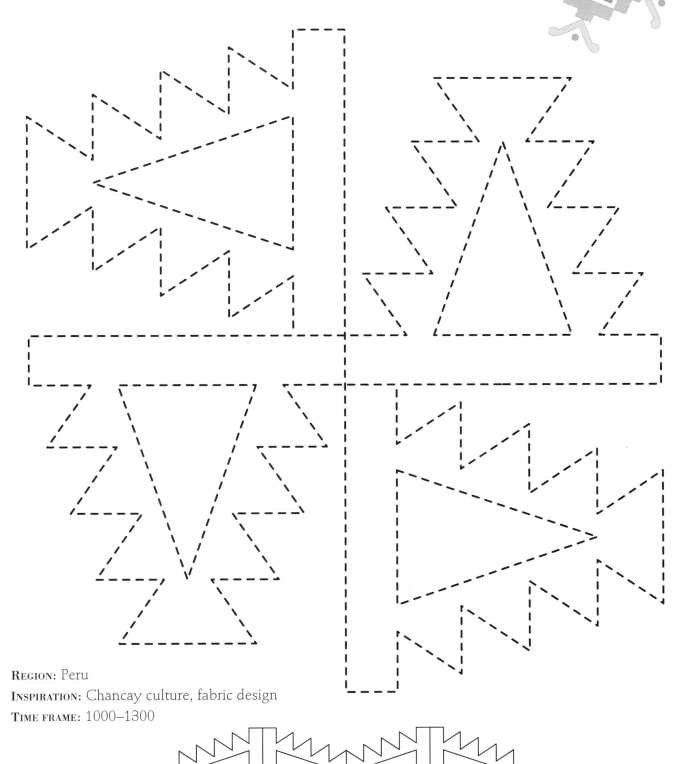

REGION: Peru

INSPIRATION: Chancay culture, fabric design

TIME FRAME: 1000–1300

Border Design

South America

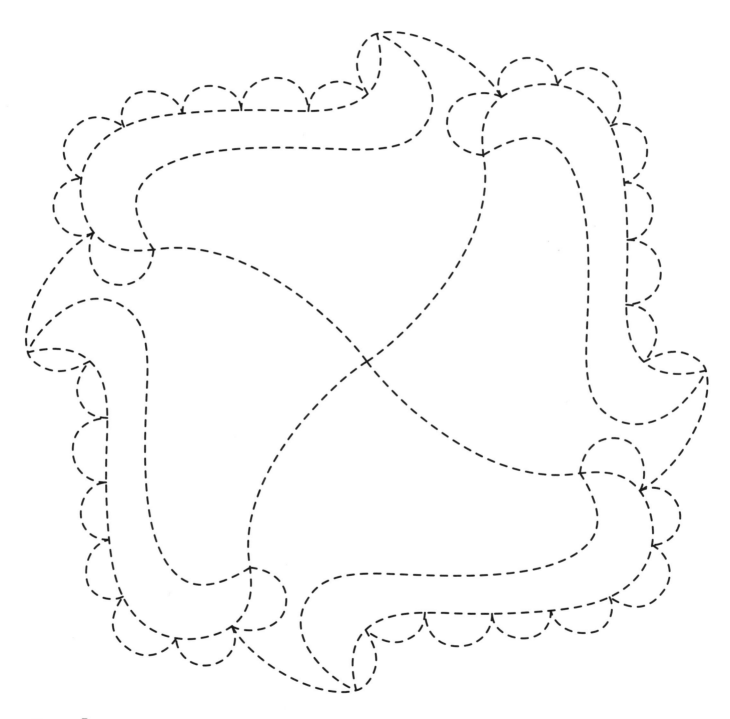

REGION: Peru

INSPIRATION: Chavín culture, pottery vase

REGION: Peru

INSPIRATION: Chincha, carved wooden ceremonial oar

TIME FRAME: 1200–1450

About the Author

Adapting motifs from different cultural items, Dr. Joyce Mori creates quilting designs and generates ideas for quilt projects. Her interest in other cultures comes from her educational training and Ph.D. in anthropology. Specializing in diverse designs and cultures, Joyce has been quilting for over 15 years.

Joyce has written over 75 articles and 13 books on quilting subjects. This is her sixth book for the American Quilter's Society. Her work has been exhibited in galleries and quilt shows, as well as public buildings and private collections.

Residing in Illinois, Joyce lives with her husband, John, and has collaborated on some quilted pieces with her adult daughter, Susan. She finds that quilting is a wonderful outlet for creative expression.